Coaching
Practice

ISBN 1 902523 71 7

sports coach UK
114 Cardigan Road
Headingley
Leeds LS6 3BJ
Tel: 0113-274 4802 Fax: 0113-275 5019
Email: coaching@sportscoachuk.org
Website: www.sportscoachuk.org

Patron: HRH The Princess Royal

Author: Andy Miles
Editor: Lucy Hyde

Produced on behalf of **sports coach UK** by

Coachwise
Coachwise Business Solutions

Business Solutions
Coachwise Ltd
Chelsea Close
Off Amberley Road
Armley
Leeds LS12 4HP
Tel: 0113-231 1310 Fax: 0113-231 9606
Email: enquiries@coachwisesolutions.co.uk
Website: www.coachwisesolutions.co.uk

scUK will ensure that it has professional and ethical values and that all its practices are inclusive and equitable.

Preface

In recent years, sport has been increasingly viewed as an invaluable tool for promoting a whole range of Government objectives, including health and well-being, education, social inclusion, crime reduction and citizenship. In addition, an increased availability of funding through sources such as the National Lottery has prompted a growth in performance-level sport and an increased desire for international sporting success. As a result, the demand for access to sporting opportunities has risen considerably.

In order for sport to meet this elevated need and play such a wide range of roles in society, qualified and knowledgeable personnel are required to manage and deliver it. The role of the sports coach in creating a safe and controlled environment for the enjoyment, participation and development of sporting opportunities is becoming progressively more apparent. It is coaches who make things happen and who make a real difference at every level; whether on the school playing fields or at major international events. There is, therefore, an increased need for people with the appropriate coaching and leadership skills to take the first steps into sports coaching.

This resource aims to help those people wishing to begin their journey into sports coaching to gain a better understanding and appreciation of what is involved. It explores the different roles, responsibilities, skills and knowledge that a coach requires in order to be an effective provider of a positive sporting experience.

Throughout the resource, there are opportunities for the reader to reflect on their learning through a series of tasks. These may also be useful for assessment purposes or for tutors delivering coaching qualifications.

This text will begin by helping the aspiring coach understand and appreciate the context and manner in which a sports coach operates. It will then progress to explore how they can establish a safe and appropriate environment in which a participant can develop, before discussing how to build and maintain an appropriate knowledge base on which to make coaching decisions. Coaching is a dynamic role and the text will seek to show how this coaching process can be applied to both the training and competition environments.

Throughout this resource, the term *coach* is intended to be inclusive of both males and females. It is important in sport, as elsewhere, that both genders have equal status and opportunities.

Although the emphasis of this resource is on coaching, it is aimed at all those who are involved in sports programmes or who want to learn more about the coaching process (eg coaches, leaders, teachers, instructors, development officers, participants, officials, administrators, volunteers, parents/carers, sport scientists, students) and those with responsibility for the organisation of sport (eg national governing bodies, local authorities, centre managers, sports clubs).

Contents

contents

The Author

Andy Miles is currently a principal lecturer at the School of Sport, PE and Recreation at the University of Wales Institute, Cardiff (UWIC). He is the Coordinator of the school's undergraduate modular scheme and Programme Leader for the Sport and Exercise Science Degree programme. Andy teaches a range of subjects, including exercise physiology, sports coaching and sports development.

As the former Head of Educational Services at **sports coach UK**, he was involved in the development and implementation of the existing **sports coach UK** workshops and their associated resources. Andy has authored several recent texts on sports coaching, including the Coaching Essentials resource, *What is Sports Coaching?* He remains an active **sports coach UK** tutor and trainer and continues to provide sports science support services to athletes and teams of all levels.

author

1.0 The Coaching Context

With the increased emphasis on sport as a vehicle for individual and social development comes a greater demand for people who can ensure that sporting experiences are enjoyable, satisfying and safe. If these sports coaches and leaders are to be seen as central to the development of sport and the fulfilment of individual potential, an appropriate support structure needs to be in place to aid their professional development.

Therefore, the organisations accountable for the management and delivery of sport have a responsibility to ensure that the people working within it are competent, experienced and suitably qualified to undertake the required roles. These organisations – **sports coach UK**, the home country sports councils, national governing bodies of sport and other key stakeholders – have recognised this need and have collectively identified a *UK Vision for Coaching*[1] in the UK to address these issues.

With this has come the aspiration that by 2012, the practice of coaching in the UK will be elevated to a *profession* and will have:

- agreed professional and ethical values and inclusive and equitable practice
- agreed national standards of competence as a benchmark at all levels
- a regulated and licensed structure
- recognition, value and appropriate funding and reward
- a culture and structure of innovation, constant renewal and continuous professional development.

Progress towards this *UK Vision for Coaching* is ongoing and significant steps forward have been made in implementing a series of recommendations identified by the Coaching Task Force. This was established following a number of suggestions made by the Government's *Plan for Sport* about the future strategic direction of coaching and coach education, to move forward in key areas of work.

chapter one

---

[1] To read or download this, please visit www.sportscoachuk.org

The following list summarises the recommendations the Coaching Task Force was asked to examine:

- An international benchmarking exercise be undertaken to compare the preparation of coaches in England with that of other countries which were deemed to have successful systems in place, and to identify good practice.
- The implementation of a National Coaching Certificate at five levels. This would be set against the national standards and be a requirement for all national governing bodies (NGBs). The feasibility of linking this to a Licence to practice.
- The feasibility of employing an additional 3,000 full-time and part-time coaches nationwide.
- A review of **sports coach UK**, to establish its role in relation to emerging recommendations.

Many new initiatives are in place to ensure coaches are aware of the professional and ethical issues associated with equitable practice. These include educational workshops, recruitment strategies targeted at under-represented populations and the adoption of a code of conduct which identifies and recognises good practice.

> Each sport needs to develop its own code, but the generic *Code of Conduct for Sports Coaches* (2001) by **sports coach UK** provides a useful guide. Available from Coachwise 1st4sport (tel 0113-201 5555 or visit www.1st4sport.com)

Currently, only a small number of coaches are able to make a living out of coaching, most of whom are likely to be associated with high-level professional sport. However, as all coaching moves towards professional status, there will be increased opportunities for appropriately qualified people to gain paid employment as coaches. As such, there will be greater recognition and reward for coaches, who are often the unseen and unrewarded people behind successful performance.

chapter one

Sports coaching is undoubtedly on the move; moving forwards towards the professional status that sport and its participants both need and deserve. However, coaching as a profession will only be as strong and effective as the individuals who are doing the job on the ground. Coaching will only have achieved its vision and completed its journey when individual coaches have completed their own journeys towards coaching excellence.

chapter one

1.1 Getting Started in Coaching

Coaching can be very rewarding, but successful coaches do not develop overnight. They acquire the necessary skills and knowledge through an ongoing process of learning, experience and personal development. An aspiring coach wishing to set out on the journey towards coaching excellence must first ask themselves a series of questions in order to gain an understanding and appreciation of what coaching is all about. These questions include:

- what is coaching?
- why do I want to coach?
- what do I want to coach?
- who do I want to coach?
- what am I expected to do as a coach?
- what knowledge and skills do I need in order to coach?
- how should I behave when coaching?

The following chapter are based on these questions and try to define the context in which a coach operates. By addressing these issues, the coach can begin to form their own coaching philosophy. This sounds rather grand, but simply, it means a set of guiding principles that reflect personal values about how coaching should be conducted and how the coach should behave when coaching. An individual's coaching philosophy reflects his or her own interpretation of good coaching practice.

1.1.1 What is Coaching?

Some people would define coaching as the act of managing a training session in which participants learn or develop skills or work towards developing an element of fitness or, within a competitive situation, providing expert input. This interpretation understates coaching, which involves more than simply being in charge of a training session or providing advice in competition.

Typically, coaching is seen as more than just a simple act. It can be viewed as a cyclical process in which a coach plans, delivers and then reviews the impact of a series of

chapter one

4

activities, sessions or programmes designed to aid a participant's development (see Figure 1). Even this interpretation is somewhat simplistic, as it does not fully acknowledge the behind-the-scenes thinking and planning or the complex development of personal relationships and communication skills necessary for the effective progress of participants.

In its broadest sense, coaching is about the development and improvement of an individual. In a sporting context, this will usually involve advancing through performance levels in a sport or acquiring and developing the skills necessary for successful performance. Coaching is also about creating a safe and appropriate environment in which sport can take place and people can learn.

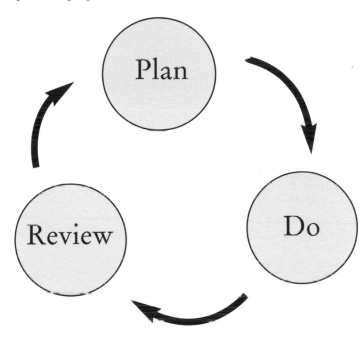

Figure 1: The cyclical coaching process

Coaching Principles

To fully appreciate and understand coaching, there is a need to recognise that a number of underpinning principles will help it have its intended impact on the participants:

- **Participant-centred** – The participant must be at the centre of the process. The coach should always start with the identification and recognition of each participant's needs when supporting, coordinating and managing the coaching process. Coaches should aim to address these needs via their coaching.
- **Empower participants** – Coaches should aim to empower participants; supporting their right to make choices, discover their own solutions and enable them to participate and develop at their own pace and in their own way, within the confines of the environment.
- **Provide opportunities** – Coaches should provide opportunities and an environment that motivates, manages risk and engenders challenge, enjoyment and, above all, achievement.
- **Build confidence** – Coaches should aim to help participants' confidence and self-esteem grow.
- **Reflect** – Coaches should reflect on their own practice and always look for ways to improve their coaching ability.

Adherence to these principles will stand coaches in good stead and ensure that their coaching practice always falls within the boundaries of good practice.

1.1.2 Why do I want to Coach?

Coaches come from all walks of life. There is no set background for a typical coach. People may choose to take up coaching because they are:

- former participants who have retired
- participants who feel they are not achieving to the best of their ability and want to remain involved in sport, but through a different avenue
- parents of children who are involved in sport
- people interested in sport who feel they have the necessary skills to be an effective coach
- sports officials or administrators who want to become involved in coaching
- people employed in a related profession (eg teachers, youth leaders, sports development officers).

Whatever their background, coaches share the same common objectives; namely, to see other people develop. However, their ultimate aspirations will vary. Some coaches are happy to work with young people to help them develop socially, gain independence and develop movement and coordination skills. However, to other coaches, this may not be sufficient. They may wish to work with elite participants and help them achieve success at a high level. Both these types of coaches have a role to play in sport, and neither one is better or more important than the other. Many coaches will gain their rewards through seeing young people develop in the long term, while others get their rewards from supporting participants in successful performance.

However, problems may arise when the coach's aspirations do not match those of their participants. Participants may not necessarily share the same reasons and motives for being involved in sport as the coach. For example, a young person may attend coaching sessions because they enjoy the social interaction with friends and learning new skills. If the performance-driven coach is always pushing for competitive success, the participant may lose interest and stop attending. Similarly, the talented individual who enjoys competition and aspires to high levels may be frustrated by a coach who spends all the time practising new skills, rather than involving players in competitions. The coach must always seek to match their motives with those of their participants. An effective coach will seek to ensure that the participant is the focus of their actions. Adopting a participant-centred approach, whereby the participant's well-being and development is seen as the main focus of the coaching process, is good practice and will inevitably be the most rewarding attitude. The coach who seeks glory for themselves will soon be disappointed.

1.1.3 What do I want to Coach?

For most coaches, *what* to coach is relatively easy to decide. They will typically coach the sport or activity they know most about or have had most experience in. Some people will argue that coaching is largely a generic process and that the skills required to coach effectively can be transferred from one sport to another. To some extent, this is true. Certain elements of coaching, such as communication, planning and building relationships, are generic and can be applied to any sport. However, as we will see later, large parts of coaching involve having the appropriate technical knowledge about a sport

to effectively analyse and compare a participant to the ideal model. An athletics coach, for example, could probably build an appropriate working relationship with a swimmer and design an appropriate fitness-training programme. However, this would have little impact in the development of the technical aspects of swimming strokes or the tumble turn, for example. Some aspects of coaching are generic and applicable to all sports, but other elements are largely specific to one sport. An effective coach will be able to apply the generic coaching principles to their instruction as well as integrate the appropriate sport-specific technical knowledge and skills into their coaching.

1.1.4 Who do I want to Coach?

Deciding who to coach will often be influenced by a coach's initial motives and reasons for coaching. For example, coaches whose focus is on development and progression are most likely to coach young people, while coaches who enjoy working towards success are more likely to work with elite-level participants. Coaches may work with different groups of participants (eg children, young people and adults) in different environments – recreational or performance – with team- or individual-based sports.

While each type of participant may pose slightly different challenges, the coach's overall approach to coaching should still remain the same; participant-centred.

Only a small number of coaches will ever be in a position to coach Olympic and world champions and reap the kind of success that famous coaches achieve. Far greater numbers will gain their rewards by seeing lower-level participants or beginners developing new skills and being successful in achieving their own personal goals.

chapter one

1 a Describe the role of a coach.

  b In pairs or in a small group, discuss, compare and contrast the roles of different coaches.

2 Describe the reasons why people coach.

3 In pairs or small groups, discuss what influences a coach's decisions in relation to:

  a who to coach

  b what level of participant to work with

  c individual or team sport

  d introducing skills to beginners or developing existing skills in established participants.

chapter one

chapter one

2.0 Coaching Responsibilities

In the sporting environment, many expectations are placed upon the coach. They will often be required to meet specific responsibilities and undertake a number of varied roles in order to fulfil these. However, coaching is meant to be a fun and rewarding activity and therefore, the expectations placed on a coach should not be too demanding. A lot of what is required is common sense and most people who start coaching will already be aware of the safety and ethical issues that exist in sport.

Coaching is essentially centred on providing an appropriate, safe and ethical environment in which participants can maximize their potential in a sport or activity. For participants to achieve their maximum potential, the coach has the responsibility to ensure that they:

- remain within the boundaries of good and acceptable practice
- create and maintain a learning environment which is safe and supportive
- provide the right resources and utilise them in the appropriate way
- establish good working relationships with all those involved
- maintain the health, safety and welfare of people involved in the session
- control the behaviour of participants and other people involved in the session.

As coaching moves towards professional status, it needs to demonstrate the ability to regulate practice. Part of this process, as is the case within any profession, whether paid or voluntary, is the need to identify accepted and established codes of conduct and practice to safeguard the welfare of the *client* (eg the athlete) and the *service provider* (eg the coach). A code of conduct in coaching is therefore essential to ensuring safe, ethical and effective coaching practice.

To assist coaches in identifying and adhering to models of good practice and meeting their responsibilities, **sports coach UK** and national governing bodies of sport have established a *Code of Conduct for Sports Coaches*[1].

chapter two

[1] **sports coach UK** (2001) *Code of Conduct for Sports Coaches.* Leeds: Coachwise Solutions. Available from Coachwise 1st4sport (tel 0113-201 5555 or visit www.1st4sport.com).

Coaches are encouraged to familiarise themselves with the key principles of the code and to follow the recommended guidelines for good practice. The key principles identified within the *Code of Conduct* are:

- **Rights – Coaches must respect and champion the rights of every individual to participate in sport**. For the coach, this means two things. Firstly, they must ensure that the coaching opportunities they provide are accessible by all and that people are not excluded on the grounds of their gender, age, race, ability, faith or sexual orientation. There are a number of ways in which this can be achieved, depending on the circumstances. It may, for example, mean ensuring that a coaching session takes place in a facility that has child care arrangements, to allow parents with children to take part. It may mean being sensitive to the different holidays that religions recognise and not expecting a participant of a particular faith to attend training on one of their recognised religious festivals. Secondly, it is a coach's responsibility to ensure that they and their participants abstain from discriminatory behaviour and language during coaching sessions. It is important to create an environment in which everybody has the opportunity to participate to the best of their ability without fear of prejudice or harassment.

- **Relationships – Coaches must develop a relationship with participants (and others) based on openness, honesty, mutual trust and respect**. The relationships a coach establishes between themself and their participants can be very important in ensuring the success of the coaching process. The key to establishing good relationships is good communication and understanding. This means maintaining openness and honesty, and respecting and trusting each other at an appropriate level. A coach will be able to get the best out of a participant when they understand how the participant thinks, behaves and responds to instructions. Similarly, a participant will be motivated to learn once they have an appreciation of the coach's style of coaching and have developed a respect for the coach's knowledge, skills and status. In developing good relationships, it is also important to empower participants to contribute to the decision-making process and to be able to voice their concerns and opinions without fear of chastisement.

A good coach must also be able to manage potential problems in their relationships. When working with young people, there is a danger that they will see the coach as a

chapter two

substitute parent. Thus, the coach's role can take on new dimensions, such as carer. In such situations, it is important to behave in an appropriate way to prevent any misinterpretation of actions. Coaches also need to be aware of, and take steps to avoid, the potential danger of developing inappropriate, and possibly abusive relationships.

While parents can be useful assets to coaches, they can also be a hindrance if they are too demanding or too protective. Maintaining parental support is important to both the coach and the young participant, so coaches must take steps to ensure that parents feel involved in their child's coaching without feeling the need to take over or undermine the coach's role.

- **Responsibilities (personal standards) – Coaches must demonstrate proper personal behaviour and conduct at all times.** Coaches should remember that they have an influential role to play and may often be viewed as a role model. To ensure that they use this influence positively, coaches should behave in an appropriate way so that participants will imitate good practice and acceptable behaviour. This should include:
  - avoiding the use of abusive language, alcohol and drugs
  - mainting equal interest in all participants
  - displaying control, dignity and professionalism
  - respecting rules and accepting officials' decisions
  - accepting defeat in a fair and sporting manner.

- **Responsibilities (professional standards) – To maximise benefits and minimise the risks to athletes, coaches must attain a high level of competence through qualifications and a commitment to ongoing training that ensures safe and correct practice.** The *UK Vision for Coaching* has identified the need for a licensed coaching structure and the creation of a culture of continual professional development. As such, coaches have a responsibility to ensure that they remain up to date with their coaching knowledge and skills. This will help to maintain a safe coaching environment and the respect of participants and colleagues.

These responsibilities relate to every aspect of coaching, and coaches have a duty to adhere to the principles outlined in order to maintain the integrity of the coaching profession, their sport and themself.

chapter two

2.1 The Roles of a Coach

Having identified the general responsibilities expected of coaches, it is now appropriate to identify some of the specific roles they may be required to undertake in the course of their careers. The following identifies and describes some of the main roles a coach may be required to assume.

Teacher, educator or instructor

These terms may be used synonymously and reflect the educational role that a coach is required to adopt. Typically, this will involve teaching participants how to do things so that they can learn and develop new techniques and skills. It will also involve teaching people when and how to use newly acquired skills; thus enabling the coach to introduce tactical and strategic issues to participants.

Aside from the technical and tactical aspects of coaching, the coach will invariably be required to teach participants emotional and social skills. This is particularly the case with coaches of young participants, who will have to teach them how to control their emotions, how to cope with winning and losing, how to develop self-esteem and self-confidence and how to work as part of a team. As sport is seen as a social vehicle to help young people learn life skills, the educational role of the coach needs to be able to facilitate a suitable environment in which young participants can experience and learn such skills.

The educational role of the coach will vary considerably according to the stage of development and experience of their participants. A coach who is introducing a new technique to a young participant who is new to a sport will need to approach the educational role in a different way than the coach working with an established participant to refine a tactical manoeuvre or set play. Coaches will therefore need to adopt different teaching styles in accordance with the different learning styles of their participants.

Trainer, fitness coach or strength and conditioning coach

This term is sometimes mistakenly used as an alternative term for a coach. However, there is a distinct difference between the broad function of a coach and the specific role of a trainer. Typically, this is associated with the development of the physical condition of

participants. All sports place some form of physical demand on participants and there is a need to ensure that participants are physically able to meet this. The coach as a trainer will therefore be expected to devise and implement a physical training programme to ensure that participants are able to maintain good all-round health and have the required levels of fitness to be able to perform effectively.

In some instances, a coach may be fortunate enough to have access to a specialist trainer or fitness and conditioning expert who is able to relieve some of the coach's duties as a trainer. However, even if somebody else is helping with the training role, the coach still needs to have an overall view on the physical and mental demands placed on their participants and be aware of how they are being trained to meet these demands.

Innovator

Coaching is about improvement and development, and an effective coach will always be looking for new and improved ways of doing things. Whether this is identifying and adopting a new drill or practice or integrating the latest scientific developments into a training programme, there is always the need to be innovative and creative. Adopting new ideas and using the latest scientific knowledge to inform practice will have many advantages. It will allow the coach to develop interesting sessions to ensure that participants remain involved and do not become bored or complacent in their training. It will also ensure participants can harness any advantages that new scientific approaches offer and reduce injury risk through the adoption of new and safe training techniques.

Motivator

Participants will develop best when they operate within a supportive environment. One of the coach's roles is to create and sustain a positive environment in both training and competition situations. Acting as a motivator during training will enable participants to gain the most from sessions and, by encouraging participants to do their best, the coach will support their learning. A learner who is constantly criticised and put down while trying to learn new skills will soon become disillusioned and ineffective as a participant. In contrast, the learner who is encouraged, supported and given regular praise for their achievements and progress, however small, will remain keen and motivated, and flourish into an effective participant.

Manager

This term may have several interpretations; all equally appropriate to the function of a coach. Firstly, it applies to the role the coach will play in managing the development of their participants through the structured management of the coaching environment, training programme and technical and tactical development of participants. An effective coach will always have a clear understanding of exactly where a participant is in terms of their personal development and will be aware of what training is required and when this needs to take place.

Secondly, in the competitive environment the coach may fulfil the role of team manager and, as such, will take on an administrative role to ensure that individuals or teams are entered for competitions, travel arrangements are made and facilities are booked. They may also select the team, make tactical decisions, manage substitutions and lead half-time team talks.

In instances where the coach is supported by other coaches, sports scientists or fitness and conditioning specialists, they will need to manage the coaching team. This will require a different set of people-management skills and will add an additional responsibility to the coach's role.

Role model

Coaches play a very important role within sport and can have a significant influence on the participants they coach. Participants will look upon their coaches as role models and seek to imitate their behaviour. It is vital, therefore, that a coach portrays a positive image, ensures their coaching is safe and responsible, and reflects behaviour which is in line with accepted good practice.

chapter two

The influence a coach can have on the development of their participants extends to a number of areas. These include the following key factors:

- **Social** – the coach can model good social behaviour and influence participants in cooperation, teamwork, citizenship, fair play and dealing with winning and losing.
- **Personal** – the coach can influence the development of various personal skills by helping participants learn life skills, promote their own welfare, manage personal matters (eg education, careers, socialising) and develop sound values and attitudes (eg self-discipline, good manners and politeness).
- **Psychological** – the coach can create appropriate environments in which participants can learn to control their emotions and develop self-esteem.
- **Health** – by providing appropriate training programmes and advice, the coach can influence the development of a good all-round healthy lifestyle and improve a participant's physical condition.

Given the amount of time a coach and their participants are likely to spend in each other's company, they will inevitably develop a working relationship. This must be based on openness, honesty, mutual trust and respect. Because of the influential position a coach occupies, it is important to live up to the participants' expectations and not abuse the trust put in them.

Fulfilling coaching roles

As has been shown, there are a variety of roles a coach is required to fulfil. The frequency and manner in which this is achieved will vary according to who is being coached and the different situations in which coaching occurs (eg training, competition, post-training/competition).

In the main, most coaching takes place away from competition and within a training environment. The coach and participant will spend large amounts of time in coaching sessions in which new techniques and skills are learned, physical fitness is developed and tactical activities, practised. It is in these situations that the coach adopts the key roles identified above. The relative emphasis placed on the different roles will shift depending on the nature of the sessions being delivered, the level, age and experience of the participants and the stage of the competitive season in which the coaching takes place.

The coach's role does not stop as soon as participants enter a competitive situation. Some coaches argue that once competition starts, the participants are on their own. This is not the case. The coach will still have a role to play, either as the tactician, motivator or advisor; or simply as the supporter.

During competition, coaches are in a good position to observe what is going on and will often see things that participants are not aware of because they are not directly involved in play. Effective coaches will use their observation and analysis skills to identify any tactical or technical errors that participants may be exhibiting. In team sports, they may have an opportunity to make changes based on their observations (eg substitutions, time-outs or intervals).

Once a training session or competition is over, the coach still has a role to play. The evaluation of what has happened and the identification of issues that need addressing form a key part of the planning for future coaching sessions. Discussing what has been achieved with participants is an important part of the evaluation process and will help shape new goals.

The job description of a coach is, as has been shown above, diverse, and the coach is expected to take on many different roles; some of them all at the same time. Appreciation of these different roles and responsibilities will allow a coach to begin to identify exactly what they need to know and be able to do in order to be an effective coach.

chapter two

2.2 Knowledge and Skills of Coaching

In order to be able to fulfil their different roles and meet the responsibilities placed on them, a coach must have a wide range of skills and a broad knowledge base on which to draw. The following chapter highlight some of the key areas in which the coach needs to be knowledgeable and address some of the important skills necessary to coach effectively.

2.2.1 Knowledge for Coaching

Having a large amount of knowledge about a specialist sport is not sufficient. Coaches need to have a wider knowledge base that allows them to understand different aspects of sport and coaching. The bank of knowledge that coaches need to have falls broadly into three categories:

- Knowledge of their sport
- Knowledge of participants
- Knowledge of factors that affect performance.

The scope of this resource does not allow for an in-depth account of all the different knowledge that is required within these different categories. Therefore, the following is an overview of some of the key elements associated with each area of knowledge.

Knowledge of their sport

In order to effectively coach a sport, coaches will need to have a good working knowledge of it. This should include both a full understanding of the techniques, skills and coaching methods that work best and a good knowledge of the rules and tactics associated with the sport.

A fundamental aspect of coaching is the introduction and teaching of new techniques. In order for a coach to be effective at this, they need to be able to introduce, explain and, if necessary, demonstrate new techniques to participants. Having done this, they must observe the learner as they practise what they have been taught. While observing, the coach must compare the learner's action with the desired action and identify any discrepancies and errors. Knowledge of the different techniques is therefore vital to the

chapter two

learning process. If a coach does not know what the correct technique should look like or what it involves, they are not going to be effective at teaching it.

A coach must also know the most effective sequence in which to introduce and coach techniques so that participants learn them effectively and correctly. Understanding the different methods of teaching and introducing techniques is important (eg the different whole-part approaches to skill acquisition; see the following panel), as is knowing when to break down a skill into its constituent components to teach it, rather than trying to teach it as a complete skill. For example, some techniques and skills are best taught in their entirety as a complete skill (eg a somersault) while others (eg a basketball lay-up shot) may be best taught by breaking them down into smaller components.

Breaking down skills

There are a variety of approaches to breaking down sports skills for the purpose of learning. If a skill is reasonably simple, it can be introduced and taught as a whole skill. In this way, all elements of the skill can be introduced at the same time without the need to identify individual components. The learner then practises the whole skill (eg a forehand shot in tennis).

However, if the skill is more complex and comprises a series of smaller elements, it may be better to introduce each of these separately. This will allow the learner to practise the different parts of the technique before trying to execute the whole skill. A good example of this could be the pole vault. A successful vault consists of a number of different elements, including gripping the pole, carrying the pole, planting the pole in the box, take-off, using the pole to lift the body, positioning the body over the bar. To try to do all this in one go would be very difficult for a beginner. An approach that allows a learner to practice each element and then to begin to put the sequence together would be more effective than practising the whole skill from the outset.

chapter two

A good knowledge of a sport will also help the coach effectively manage the rate of progression of learning, to ensure that participants learn at an appropriate and safe rate. The introduction of complex skills too early into a coaching programme may mean that participants are unable to successfully perform these and they may become demotivated, bored or, in extreme cases, injured as a result of incorrect technique. Coaches should limit the range of different techniques, skills and tactics that are introduced, or participants may struggle to make the right choice at the required time. As participants' abilities improve, the range of options can be increased.

An effective coach will therefore be able to analyse techniques, skills and tactics, and help the participants learn and practise them. If a coach performs this role effectively, participants will become self-reliant and independent. They will learn how and when to use different techniques, and how to choose the correct tactics and skills for a variety of situations.

A coach who has some experience of participating within a sport is likely to be able to appreciate the demands of that sport and be aware of the technical and tactical issues to a greater extent than a person who has limited experience of a sport. This does not mean that to be a successful coach someone has to have been a successful performer, but does highlight the need for a good understanding and appreciation of a sport in order to be able to coach it effectively.

Coaches are advised to consult additional materials relating to the knowledge specific to their sport and should contact their national governing body for more details.

Knowledge of participants

Getting to know participants and how they learn is a significant aspect of coaching. Knowing the individual personalities and characteristics of participants will help a coach develop and structure sessions to meet the needs of individuals. Every person is different and some prefer to learn in certain ways, while others prefer different approaches. An understanding of the different ways in which people learn will help the coach create effective learning environments for his participants.

People learn best when:

- their interest and motivation is maintained
- they are actively involved in their learning
- they are able to build on previous experiences
- they are able to see things fit together
- they can see improvements in their performance.

In addition to knowing how people learn new skills, a coach needs to understand how participants develop physically and mentally. This is particularly relevant for the coach of young participants. Children and young people grow and develop at different rates, so this will impact on how they perform and respond to training. A coach needs to be aware of the different factors associated with physical development in order to effectively manage the training loads and demands placed on young participants. Placing too much physical load on young people while they are not fully developed can lead to injury, illness or withdrawal from sport.[1]

Knowing how to guide and motivate participants to enjoy sport, control anxiety, cope with success and failure, achieve personal goals and fulfil their potential is also important for a coach. Coaches should seek to provide positive experiences for participants. A good knowledge of the different ways in which people learn, develop and deal with emotions will help the structuring of sessions.

Knowledge of factors affecting performance

A good knowledge of how the mind and body respond to exercise and training and how to promote and support a healthy lifestyle is of great benefit to the coach. Training participants to be able to meet the mental and physical demands placed on them during training and competition is a fundamental aspect of coaching. Not only will an appropriate level of physical and mental fitness ensure that participants are able to train and compete to the best of their ability, but it will also help to reduce the risk and prevalence of injury.

Developments in the academic study of sport and sports science have led to a greater understanding of how the mind and body work during exercise. The application of sports science knowledge to coaching is now commonplace and sports scientists and coaches are

chapter two

[1] Stratton, G. (2004) *BASES Guidelines for Resistance Exercise*. Leeds: Coachwise Business Solutions. Available from Coachwise 1st4sport (tel 0113-201 5555 or visit www.1st4sport.com).

able to work together to address a number of the problems and issues facing participants. For example, an understanding of how the human body stores and releases energy has allowed coaches to gain a better understanding of how participants can resist fatigue, and thus enhance performance, through sensible nutritional practices and appropriate fluid and energy intake before, during and after training and competition.

While a coach is not expected to have an in-depth understanding of all the components of sports science, the coach should at least have a working knowledge of some of the major aspects. They should also be aware of where participants can go to gain more advanced advice and help in this area. The prevalence of practising sports scientists across the UK means that the opportunity to apply the fundamentals of sports science to coaching are now available to coaches at all levels, and not just at the elite level.

In terms of understanding and integrating sports science knowledge into coaching, the coach should endeavour to know:

- how the body works
- the effects of training on the efficiency of the body
- how the mind works and how mental skills can be improved
- how to utilise technology to observe and analyse sporting techniques and performance
- how to construct training sessions that will develop these elements.

chapter two

2.2.2 Coaching Skills

While having the knowledge identified above is important, it is of little use to the coach if they do not have the appropriate skills to be able to apply it to their coaching. The skills required by a coach fall into four broad categories:

1 Management
2 Organisation
3 Communication
4 Teaching.

chapter two

Management skills

As has been shown previously, the role of the coach includes managing the coaching environment and acting as a role model to inspire and guide participants in their quest for improved performance. To achieve this, the coach has to demonstrate good leadership and management skills through:

- ensuring that participants are well organised in what they say and do
- effectively managing and directing participants and appropriate others within the coaching environment
- effectively and safely managing and coordinating the use of equipment and facilities
- delivering safe and well-structured sessions
- providing guidance and support to participants
- establishing and maintaining good communication channels with participants and appropriate others within the coaching environment.

A major part of being a good manager is an ability to motivate participants. An effective coach should not need to specifically motivate their participants (eg by providing them with interesting tasks), as they will have created a coaching environment which encourages self-motivation. Participants will usually be self-motivated if they operate within an environment that enables them to:

- enjoy their coaching sessions and have fun
- share experiences with others and socialise with friends
- compete in a safe and non-threatening environment
- meet new challenges
- keep fit and healthy
- achieve success or gain a reward (eg a personal-best performance or a trophy)
- please others and receive praise (eg parents and friends)
- create a positive self-image
- achieve goals and realise their dreams.

The key to being an effective motivator of participants is to understand their motives for participating and to know their desired goals. Establishing a good relationship with participants in order to identify what makes them want to be involved in sport is essential.

Organisation skills

A coach should always remember that sound planning and good organisation are essential to the smooth and effective running of coaching sessions and programmes. Throughout the entire coaching process, there is a need for the coach to be well organised. Even before a coaching session or programme begins, a coach needs to put their planning and organising skills into action. This will ensure that they:

- have effectively identified a set of goals for the session or programme
- are aware of the resources available for the sessions
- know sufficient information about the participants
- have developed a plan that will ensure participants achieve the desired goals.

Once a session gets underway, the coach needs to make sure that they are suitably organised to ensure participants are doing the right thing, in the right place, at the right time.

An integral part of the effective organisation of coaching sessions and programmes is to have appropriate administrative skills. Creating good coaching plans and keeping records of what participants have achieved in previous sessions is important. Most coaches will not enjoy the administrative side of coaching but recognise that without it, the coaching process will fall down. Imagine trying to run a coaching session if the facility has not been booked. This may be one area where the effective coach could utilise the skills of others. Perhaps parents or partners, or the participants themselves, could take some responsibility for some administrative aspects of the coaching role. If a coach does choose to devolve this responsibility to another person, they need to ensure that whoever takes on the role is able to demonstrate the standards and behaviour required to set positive examples to the participants.

Communication skills

Effective coaches are always good communicators. They will demonstrate the ability to convey their thoughts and ideas to others in an effectual manner and be able to communicate with participants, parents, officials and others involved in sport.

chapter two

Good communication, however, is not simply about talking and telling people what to do or what you think. It is about knowing when to speak, how to get a message across and when to listen. Communication is a two-way process involving both the sending of a message and the receiving of that message. The coach has to:

- **be able to send messages effectively** – this can involve the use of both verbal and non-verbal communication and requires a coach to identify the most appropriate method for sending a message to a participant. In many instances, the spoken word is the most effective means of delivering a message, but a coach has to remember that the message may get lost if too many words are used, or the words are delivered in an inappropriate way. Talking too much can confuse a participant and, more often than not, a simple short set of instructions or piece of advice is more effective than a prolonged monologue. Similarly, the pace, tone and volume of the spoken word is important. A coach who is constantly shouting abuse at a participant will soon lose their interest and fail to deliver the message. Finding the right balance for delivering the spoken word is the key to good use of verbal communication.

  On some occasions, messages may not need to be conveyed through the spoken word. Non-verbal communication can be as effective; if not more so, in some instances. This form of communication may involve gestures, facial expressions, body language or some other form of signalling. Coaches tend not to be as good at using non-verbal communication to convey thoughts and feelings as they are at using the spoken word to convey their message, but the impact can be significant. A well-placed smile or thumbs up to a participant who has just executed a technique correctly can be enough to get the message across.

- **be able to receive incoming messages** – this is about listening and interpreting the signs and signals of others. A good coach will be able to glean large amounts of information from participants by listening to their opinions and comments. Understanding how a participant feels about a particular activity or drill will help the coach identify whether that drill is appropriate or not.

- **be able to check that messages have been received correctly** – this is all about questioning and checking for understanding. A good coach will be able to question their participants to check that they have understood what they have been told. If a

participant is unable to identify correctly what they are required, they may not have received the message or understood what is required. Many people will automatically assume that, if a message has not been received correctly, it is the fault of the receiver. This may not be the case, as it may well have been the initial message or the way in which it was sent that was inappropriate. A good coach will check their participants' understanding by asking them to confirm understanding or to paraphrase the message that they think they have been sent. If necessary, the coach will then find alternative ways to convey the message.

Teaching skills

To introduce and teach new techniques and skills, coaches need to be able to draw on their knowledge of how people learn. They will need to structure activities and practices in a way that allows participants to progress through the different stages of learning at a pace that is appropriate to them. This will involve structuring coaching sessions so that appropriate time is allocated to the different stages of introducing new techniques and skills. Therefore, a session should include time for the coach to:

- **introduce** and **explain** the technique to be learned
- **demonstrate** how the technique should be performed
- allow participants to **practise** the technique
- **observe** and **analyse** the participants as they practise
- **identify** and **correct** errors.

Good coaches will be able to maximise their participants' learning by making appropriate choices about what, how and when to teach a particular skill or technique. It is important to progress in short, simple, logical steps from one part of the session to the next and at a pace which suits most of the participants.

Acquiring and maintaining knowledge and skills

The previous chapter have introduced the key knowledge and skills that a coach requires in order to be effective. These cannot be acquired overnight. However, a coach has to work on their skills and develop their knowledge base over time. The best way to develop the appropriate knowledge and skills for coaching is through coaching itself. Continued practice and constant evaluation of coaching will help a coach to become more effective.

chapter two

The learning process can, however, be supported through:

- regular contact and discussion with other coaches
- working with a mentor (eg another qualified and experienced coach)
- reading coaching resources
- reviewing material from other sports
- attending coach education courses to gain or upgrade coaching qualifications
- becoming a member of a coaching organisation
- the development of a personal continual professional development programme.

It is unlikely that any coach will ever reach the point where they know and can do everything, because the knowledge and skills required for effective coaching is constantly changing and developing. The *UK Vision for Coaching* recognises the importance of staying up to date with coaching knowledge by encouraging coaches to be part of a culture and structure of innovation, constant renewal and continuous professional development.

Keeping knowledge and skills up to date will help a coach continue to provide a safe coaching environment and maintain the respect of their participants and fellow coaches.

2.3 Good Practice; Coaching Effectively

As we have seen previously, there are certain expectations placed on a coach. One of these is that they will behave safely, responsibly and ethically. The way in which a coach behaves will reflect their general attitude to coaching and, in the modern coaching environment, there is a need to ensure that the behaviours elicited by a coach are in line with acceptable good practice. As mentioned previously, the coaching profession would wish to see *professional and ethical values and inclusive and equitable practice*. Thus, there is an expectation that coaches will behave in a way that reflects this.

It would be inappropriate to suggest that there is only one correct way to coach. There are many different ways in which safe, responsible and ethical coaching can be achieved. Many different ways of coaching are recognised, but it is too simplistic to categorise them as distinct styles. Rather, there is a range of behaviours and approaches that coaches draw

chapter two

upon in their coaching. An effective coach is able to draw on the appropriate set of behaviours according to the context in which they are operating.

Most coaches suggest that coaching should always be participant-centred. In this way, the participant has some involvement in the decision-making process and is actively encouraged to take a part in their own learning. This will involve some degree of empowerment of the individual. Adopting a participant-centred approach usually involves the coach providing leadership, offering guidance, sharing decision-making and guiding participants towards selecting and achieving their personal goals. Styles of coaching that reflect this participant-centred approach are often termed **democratic** because there is an element of discussion and agreement in the decision-making process.

This approach, however, is only effective if the participant is at the appropriate stage of development, both technically and cognitively, to be able to take responsibility for their own learning. In instances where the participant is not able, or willing, to be involved in this, the coach may need to adopt a more **coach-driven** approach.

Such an approach will involve the coach making most of the decisions on behalf of the participants and giving clear, direct and confident commands. This may be particularly appropriate when working with young or inexperienced participants, or in situations where safety is a critical factor. This approach to coaching is often termed **autocratic** because only the coach is involved in the decision-making.

The way in which an individual chooses to coach will be influenced by a number of factors. These include the following:

- **Coaching motives** – the reasons why people take up coaching will undoubtedly affect the way in which they coach. The coach who wishes to see young people develop socially and learn new skills will adopt a supportive, educational approach to coaching and place an emphasis on personal development rather than competitive success. For other, more competitive-driven coaches, the emphasis may be on the development of tactics and competitive spirit. Different coaches will have different indicators of success and, as a result, they will probably end up working with different types of participants.

chapter two

- **The participants** – if a coach is to adopt a participant-centred approach as is recommended, they should adapt their coaching style to meet the specific needs of their participants.
- **The situation** – There are some situations in which a particular style of coaching is more appropriate than another. In certain contexts, for example, where safety is an important issue, it might be more appropriate to adopt an autocratic and instructional approach to coaching in order to maintain control and ensure that accidents do not happen and participants behave in an appropriate manner.
- **Personality** – coaches are human beings and thus have individual personalities. Some coaches may be extroverted, outgoing and lively in their approach to coaching while others may be more introverted and go about their coaching in a quiet, calm manner. In truth, personality does not matter, provided appropriate actions and behaviours are maintained.
- **Knowledge** – The more knowledgeable coach will adopt a different approach to their coaching than the coach who lacks knowledge in certain areas. A coach lacking in knowledge may come across as low in confidence and may be perceived as lacking in innovation skills as they may not know how to deal with certain situations.

As we have seen above, the context in which a coach operates exists as a result of a number of issues and principles. A coach has to seek to identify their own answers to the what, why, and how questions associated with coaching and create their own set of beliefs and styles to utilise during coaching.

Once a coach has established a philosophy about how they are going to coach, they need to begin to develop an understanding of the issues and actions involved in the coaching process. This will be introduced in Chapter 3.0.

chapter two

1 List the skills of a coach.

2 List and describe five roles of a coach.

3 Produce a list of the key rights, relationships and responsibilities of a coach and suggest how these might influence their behaviour and coaching style. Note: **You might like to obtain a copy of a sport's code of conduct or the sports coach UK *Code of Conduct for Sports Coaches* to assist you**[1].

4 List the different methods a coach can use to communicate with participants.

5 Using specific examples, explain the difference between verbal and non-verbal communication.

6 In pairs or in a group, discuss what you consider to be the features of effective communication in coaching.

7 In pairs or in a group, describe the knowledge a coach requires to be safe and effective.

8 Describe how a coach can be participant-centred in their approach to coaching.

chapter two

---

[1] **sports coach UK** (2001) *Code of Conduct for Sports Coaches.* Leeds: Coachwise Solutions. Available from Coachwise 1st4sport (tel 0113-201 5555 or visit www.1st4sport.com).

3.0 The Coaching Process

Coaching is typically described as a dynamic process whereby a coach plans a coaching session or a series of sessions, delivers and then reviews the session(s) in order to inform future planning. This forms the plan, do, review cycle of events identified on page 5.

In reality, coaching is about more than the simple mechanistic approach suggested by this model. Coaching is centred around the interaction between coaches and participants, the personal development of individuals and the intrinsic and extrinsic rewards that performance development can offer both the participant and the coach. However, the conceptual complexities of coaching are beyond the scope of this resource and it is sufficient here to explore in detail the different elements of the coaching process in order to fully appreciate exactly what a coach must do to ensure effective performance development.

The coaching process can be broken down into a number of different elements and these typically occur in a cyclical order in line with the broader plan, do, review stages of the process. The coaching process includes the following elements:

- **Planning for participant development:**
  - Collecting and analysing relevant information
  - Identifying participant needs
  - Goal-setting
  - Identifying appropriate resources
  - Identifying appropriate activities to enable goals to be achieved
  - Planning coaching sessions/programmes.

- **Delivering effective coaching sessions:**
  - Preparing the coaching environment
  - Starting a coaching session
  - Managing a coaching session
  - Observation
  - Analysis
  - Planning the next activity
  - Monitoring how well the session is going
  - Concluding a coaching session.

chapter three

- **Reviewing the effectiveness of a session/series of sessions:**
  - Reviewing participant progress
  - Reviewing progress against session aims
  - Reviewing coach effectiveness
  - Identifying future participant needs
  - Identifying future coaching needs
  - Informing the planning process.

3.1 Planning for Participant Development

Undoubtedly the most significant element of the entire coaching process is the planning aspect. If a coach does not take the time to plan what they are going to do then they will get themselves into all sorts of problems later on and will struggle to maintain effective delivery.

Planning for coaching is very much like planning for a journey. A coach needs to initially work with their participants to answer the following questions:

- **Where are they now?** What is their starting point?
- **Where do they want to be?** What are their aspirations?
- **How are they going to get there?** What needs to be done?
- **What resources are available?** What facilities, equipment and activities can be used?
- **How will they know they are there?** What are the indicators of success?

Identifying a starting point is about getting to know the participants. In some instances, a coach may know a little about the participants already because they may have worked with them before. However, in other instances, a coach might be meeting a participant or group for the first time. It is important that the coach takes some time to collect and analyse relevant information about the participants in order to be adequately informed about them.

chapter three

To plan an effective coaching session or series of sessions for participants, a coach will need to identify:

- the number of participants likely to be in the group
- the age of the participants
- the gender of the participants
- the level of experience and ability of the participants
- whether the participants have any special or specific requirements.

Each of these factors will have an impact on a coaching session, as a coach's planning will differ depending on the number, age, gender mix, ability and experience of their participants. With this information, the coach has a base on which to begin planning a coaching programme. Taking time at the beginning of a coaching session to find out this information will make planning easier in the longer term.

Having identified the starting point for the coaching journey, a coach needs to identify where the desired destination is. They will need to ascertain whether the participants are simply seeking personal development in a sport through improving their understanding and skills in it, or whether they are aiming for a high level of performance and associated success. The nature of the coaching will be strongly influenced by the aspirations of the participants. In addition to this, a coach must also explore the needs of the participants. For example, mastery of the basic techniques and skills of a sport is needed before a participant can aspire to high levels of performance. Structuring a coaching programme to achieve a high level of performance without the successful attainment of the basic techniques and skills will not be effective. When seeking to identify the ultimate destination of the coaching journey, a coach must take into account what the participants wish to achieve and what they actually need in order to achieve it.

This element of the planning stage is about identifying coaching goals. Typically, setting goals within coaching is best described by the acronym SMART. This determines that coaching goals should be:

- **S** Specific – goals should be focused on a specific objective rather than being general in nature. To become a better player would be too general a goal whereas to improve the serve-volley aspect of the game is more specific. A specific goal has a much greater chance of being accomplished than a general goal.
- **M** Measurable – there has to be a means by which the progress towards a goal can be measured, otherwise how does a participant know if they have been successful? Measuring their progress helps participants to stay on track, reach their targets, and experience the positive feelings of achievement
- **A** Agreed – goals should be agreed between the coach and participant to reinforce and focus progress.
- **R** Realistic – as well as being achievable, a goal has to be realistic in that a participant has to be able to believe that he can attain it.
- **T** Time-phased – when setting goals, a coach should give an indication of when the goal is likely to be achieved by; there should be a target time for attainment of the goal.

The identification of coaching goals should be based on the needs and aspirations of the participants and an effective coach will involve the participants themselves in the identification of these goals. A participant-centred approach to coaching would advocate that the coaching goals are discussed, negotiated and agreed between the coach and the participants.

The use of goal-setting as a means of beginning the planning process is important and will help the coach shape what is to come throughout the coaching programme. Coaches should seek to establish both short-term and long-term goals. Short-term goals may be specific objectives to be achieved within a single coaching session or series of sessions, while long-term goals may reflect what the participants are seeking to achieve over the course of a season. In the planning process, the coach may therefore identify short-term goals. These should represent the building blocks or stepping stones towards the

chapter three

longer-term goals set jointly by the coach and participants. Progress towards these long-term goals can be measured by the successful attainment of the short-term goals.

Before a coach can begin to identify what they are going to do in their coaching sessions, they will need to consider what resources are available for use. The resources required for effective coaching sessions typically fall into three categories:

1   **Coaching environment** – a coach will need to know whether the appropriate facilities and space are available for their planned coaching session. Some coaches will use the same location on a regular basis and will therefore be aware of what is available and whether other people use adjacent spaces. However, there may be times when a coach is required to use a facility for the first time. **Good planning** would suggest that the coach would visit this location in advance to get an appreciation of the space and facilities available. An effective coach will plan a coaching session with the facilities and space in mind. Only a poorly organised coach would plan a coaching session to develop basketball shooting skills, for instance, and turn up to find that there are no basketball nets in the sports hall.

2   **Equipment** – A good coach would expect to plan a coaching session based on knowledge of the equipment available. For example, the effectiveness of a session designed to develop ball control skills in hockey is dependant on the availability of appropriate numbers of hockey sticks and hockey balls. A well-organised coach would ensure that sufficient balls and sticks were available to allow all participants to fully engage in the session.

3   **Human resources** – Some coaches may be fortunate enough to have other coaches available to work with them. If this is the case, the session plan needs to take this into account and coaches need to address a series of questions in their planning. These questions might include:

    -   what are the other coaches going to do
    -   how are they going to be utilised effectively within the session
    -   are they competent and qualified to take on particular roles?

Some sessions may draw on the input of other non-coaching specialists (eg sports scientists, conditioning specialists). If this is the case, again, the session plan needs to

chapter three

identify exactly how these people are expected to function by addressing certain issues:

- Are they going to working with the whole group, just some of the group or one person at a time?
- What is the rest of the group going to be doing while some are working with the specialist?
- What role does the coach play?

Having a clear identification of the starting point of the participants, a knowledge of the desired goals for a coaching programme and awareness of what resources are available will help the coach structure the journey appropriately. The coach will be able to identify exactly what is required within the coaching sessions to take participants from where they are to where they want to be.

This aspect of the planning phase will require the coach to draw on their knowledge, skills and experiences to identify exactly what technical, physical and mental developments are required to help the participants develop and achieve their desired objectives. A coach will need to decide upon and select the most appropriate coaching activities to help participants to achieve the stated goals. When planning and constructing coaching sessions, a coach will need to consider:

- what techniques and skills the participants need to learn and which activities, drills and practices will best support this learning
- the different learning styles of the participants and how the coach can create the most appropriate learning environment to facilitate learning
- the physical fitness needs of the participants and the most appropriate fitness training procedures to develop fitness levels
- the psychological requirements of participants and the most appropriate mental skills training to develop mental toughness
- any additional scientific support that may be necessary to sustain participant development
- how to construct a series of coaching sessions that help participants develop towards achieving their long-term goals
- how to balance the needs of individuals with the overall needs of a group.

chapter three

Armed with information about the participants, their goals, the available resources and the type of activities that can be used for participant development, the coach should be able to plan and construct a coaching programme and plan the constituent coaching sessions to help participants achieve the stated goals.

task three

1 In pairs or a small group, discuss the factors for consideration when planning coaching sessions.

2 a List all the things a coach needs to know about a participant or group of participants in order to plan a coaching session for them.

  b List the resources a coach requires to allow the session to begin.

3 Taking into consideration the information gathered from Tasks 1 and 2, develop a set of coaching goals for a coaching session. (Remember to make the goals *SMART*.)

4 Develop a coaching session plan based on the information gathered in Tasks 1–3.

chapter three

3.2 Delivering Effective Coaching Sessions

Once planned and prepared, a coaching programme needs to be implemented. This should be done through the delivery of a series of coherent coaching sessions. These sessions need to be delivered in a way that is consistent with good coaching practice and take into account all the elements associated with the different roles, responsibilities and behaviours identified previously.

To deliver effective coaching sessions, coaches should:

- ensure that the coaching environment and the participants are adequately prepared
- introduce and initiate planned activities
- help participants improve their performance
- manage the behaviour of participants and other staff
- work with the participants to evaluate their progress
- monitor and refine the session as it develops
- summarise and conclude the coaching session.

3.2.1 Preparing the Coaching Environment

Coaching sessions can only be effective if the environment in which they occur is safe and conducive to participant development and if positive working relationships exist between the coaches, the participants and others involved in the session. To ensure the coaching environment is appropriately prepared, a coach must:

- have identified a session plan and be aware of how this fits with the overall goals of the participants
- identify any risks that may affect the delivery of the session
- ensure that the resources and activities to be used are safe and in line with health and safety requirements and good coaching practice
- create an appropriate learning environment
- communicate information about the session to participants and other staff.

We have already discussed the importance of planning a session, so an effective coach will arrive at a session with a clear plan of action and will know exactly what the session's aims

chapter three

are, how they are going to be achieved and how they fit with the participants' long-term goals.

The first step in putting this plan into action requires the coach to check the safety of the coaching environment and identify any risks. The potential health and safety issues and risks fall into three categories:

- **The venue/coaching environment** – Coaches need to make sure that they are familiar with the normal operating and emergency procedures for the place where the sessions take place. This would include being aware of the location of emergency telephones, exits and alarms as well as first-aid kits, ambulance access points and fire marshalling locations. In addition to this emergency information, coaches should consider whether the venue is appropriate for the size of the group and the nature of the activities that are planned.

- **The equipment** – Coaches should always ensure that the equipment they use is in good working order and that they know how to carry, lift, set up and use it correctly. In addition, participants need to be instructed in the safe use of the equipment and be made aware that misbehaviour and misuse of equipment can lead to serious injury.

- **The participants** – Participants should be advised that their behaviour could potentially be a risk to their well-being and enjoyment of a coaching session. They need to be made aware of the health and safety procedures that they should follow throughout the session. It is also important that a coach ensures the participants wear appropriate clothing to maximise safety, comfort and effective attainment of a skill. In addition, the coach needs to be aware that the physical and psychological capabilities of the participants may affect safety and thus influence the content and structure of a session. For example, if a rugby session includes young people of different sizes and strengths, there may be inherent safety risks in certain tackling and scrummaging activities due to the imbalance in physical development.

As we have seen before, a key element of effective coaching is the creation of an appropriate learning environment in which participants can acquire new skills or techniques and improve their performance. To establish such an environment, a coach needs to adopt a style of coaching that creates an atmosphere where participants – particularly new participants and children – are able to feel welcome and at ease.

chapter three

The manner in which a coach introduces a session to the participants is an important element of this. Participants need to be informed about what they are expected to do and to be reassured that they will be given the full support and encouragement of the coach as they try to learn new skills. Coaches need to remind their participants that they will be operating in an environment which is open, honest and non-judgmental and that they will not be laughed at or criticised for making mistakes. This aspect of preparation will give the coach an opportunity to practise their communication skills. Good communication about the purpose and aims of a coaching session will help relax the participants and prepare them for it.

Establishing ground rules for behaviour is a good way to facilitate the development of a positive learning environment. For example, the coach may encourage their group to agree on the procedure for starting sessions (eg should there be a warm-up, or should the group be warmed up and ready to start the session at the agreed time? What should be the rule if someone arrives late?). Involving the participants in this process will give them ownership of the rules and thus make these easier to uphold. The development of such rules will create a productive coaching environment in which to inform the participants of the acceptable boundaries and alert them to any safety procedures that must be adhered to.

Participants also need to be physically prepared for a session and there is plenty of research evidence to suggest that a series of low intensity warm-up activities at the start of a session will help prepare participants physically and mentally for what is to follow. A warm-up will physically prepare the body for exercise by increasing the heart rate and enhancing blood flow to the working muscles, increasing the body and muscle temperature towards its optimal functioning level and helping muscles and nerves prepare for activity. A light physical warm-up can also give the coach an indication of the participants' levels of experience, ability and physical readiness to take part in a session and can reduce the risk of injury. An effective warm-up will include:

- low-intensity, whole-body, aerobic exercise to increase heart rate and elevate body temperature
- light, controlled stretching of all the major muscle groups and joints to prepare muscles for activity
- low intensity sports-specific activities to aid nerve conductance and muscle contractile processes.

chapter three

3.2.2 Managing the Coaching Session

Once a coaching session gets underway, the coach will need to make sure that everything is running to plan and that participants are gaining the maximum benefit from the activities. To achieve this, activities need to be introduced effectively, be well structured and well managed.

When initiating a new activity, the coach should use clear verbal instructions to **introduce** and **explain** it and supplement this with effective **demonstration**. Coaches should be able to provide explanations and demonstrations that are technically correct according to the definition of their sport or activity. Insufficient or inaccurate information can leave the participant unsure of what is required, while too much explanation could leave them confused; both have potential implications for the safe execution of an activity. The coach should therefore strike an effective balance between verbal instruction and visual demonstration. This balance of activity, instruction and discussion should be established based on the participants' age, level of experience, ability and needs. It is also important for the coach to recognise the different ways and rates at which individuals learn and ensure that an effective balance is maintained between an individual's needs and the needs of the rest of the group.

Once an activity has been introduced, a coach should allow participants to **practise** it and should use questioning and observation to check the participants' understanding of what is required. At this point, the coach should be looking to **observe** and **analyse** performance with a view to correcting any errors. This observation should involve the coach utilising their knowledge and understanding of the different techniques and skills required in their sport to compare the participants' performance of a technique with the desired ideal. Effective coaching demands that coaches should have a well-developed ability to identify the differences between how a participant executes a technique or skill and how that technique or skill should be performed.

Improving performance is then about analysing these differences and identifying appropriate interventions to correct the errors and help the participants refine their skills. A coach's ability to analyse their participants' performance depends largely on their use of questioning, the appropriate use of feedback and effective observation techniques.

chapter three

There is no substitute for practise. A coaching session in which participants are given ample time to practise what they have been taught will be more effective at developing techniques than one which is dominated by instruction and demonstration by the coach. Coaches should therefore ensure that they provide sufficient time in their sessions for participants to practise new techniques and to achieve the required level according to their own pace and learning ability. Coaches should not try to achieve too much in a session or rush on from one activity to another without giving participants time to practise what they have been taught.

Effective management of a coaching session is all about finding the right balance between instructions, demonstrations and practice. If the balance is not achieved then participants will either become bored and disinterested because there is too much talk by the coach and not enough practical opportunities for them or they will become demotivated by not having sufficient time to experience success as a result of the coach giving limited practice time before moving on to another activity. Coaches should therefore select a range of appropriate activities and make their sessions interesting and varied; not boring and repetitive. This will maintain the participants' interest as well as help them achieve their desired goals.

In order to maintain an appropriate learning environment throughout a coaching session, an effective coach will be able to:

- establish a positive and goal-oriented relationship with their participants
- communicate with their participants in an appropriate way
- listen to and negotiate with the participants
- adapt their coaching and motivational styles to meet the ongoing coaching situation and the needs of the participants
- facilitate and encourage fun and enjoyment
- minimise disruption in the session and the likelihood of injuries
- encourage and reinforce positive behaviour.

Most coaches enjoy the delivery elements of the coaching process, but some can be so wrapped up in the identification and correction of errors that they lose sight of the session goals. Being able to keep a coaching session on track and according to plan while still delivering effectively is a formidable task and requires great skill. Managing an effective

chapter three

session is like juggling – there is a need to keep an eye on all elements and to do lots of different things at the same time. Checking progress against the session plan and the session goals as the session continues is important.

There will inevitably be occasions when the coach needs to stray from the original plan; either because participants have not fully understood or mastered a technique or an activity that a coach has introduced, or they have progressed quicker than the coach had envisaged. To deal with this, a good coach will always have a contingency plan that they can draw on. This might include additional activities that may help participants develop a technique and give them different practice opportunities or may include more advanced alternatives that some or all of the group can be introduced to if they have progressed quicker than intended. Managing change effectively within a coaching session is therefore an important coaching skill, as is being flexible and able to think of new alternatives while still managing the session.

3.2.3 Summarising and Concluding Coaching Sessions

Ideally, the practical aspects of a coaching session should end with some opportunity for the participants to practise what they have learned within a realistic setting. A match or short tournament with particular emphasis on the techniques introduced is a good way of allowing participants to integrate their new knowledge into a realistic context. This might be followed by a cool-down, which will serve to physically prepare the participants to end the session and to reduce the risk of muscle stiffness or injury. A cool-down will typically involve similar activities to a warm-up, but with an emphasis on a gradual reduction in exercise intensity.

A coaching session should then conclude with a summary of what has been learned. This would typically involve revisiting the session goals and checking whether the participants and the coach feel that they have been successfully achieved. This will help the coach gather information to inform the planning of subsequent sessions and reinforce any key learning points for the participants.

chapter three

Gaining feedback from participants as to how they feel the session has gone is also useful, as it will:

- help the coach to re-establish goals and set new ones for subsequent sessions
- aid the coach in refining and improving the activities used
- help reinforce what a participant has learned
- motivate the participant to attend future sessions
- facilitate a coach's self-reflection.

At the end of a session, a coach must also take responsibility for:

- ensuring that participants are appropriately informed about future sessions and/or future events
- encourage continued practice and future participation
- checking the venue and the equipment following use and putting equipment away if required
- supervising the departure of participants; in particular, children
- leaving the coaching environment in a fit state for future use.

chapter three

1 Describe the important issues that a coach needs to be aware of when delivering a session.

2 a In pairs or a small group, identify and discuss any risks that may affect the delivery of a coaching session.

b Discuss potential health and safety issues and how a coach can reduce these.

3 Explain what a coach should do when delivering a coaching session.

4 Identify and describe the methods a coach may use to maintain an appropriate learning environment.

5 Describe the benefits of a coach gaining feedback from participants about the coaching session.

6 Describe the roles and responsibilities of the coach at the end of the coaching session.

chapter three

3.3 Reviewing Your Coaching

Coaching does not stop once the participants have gone home and the equipment is put away. Effective coaches are always trying to improve what they do. This involves them in thinking about and reviewing the coaching sessions they have delivered in order to identify strengths and weaknesses and to learn lessons for the future. It is important for a coach to spend some time reviewing what has gone on in a coaching session and this process of reviewing sessions should help to inform the planning of subsequent sessions.

When reviewing a coaching session, a coach should seek to:

- collect, analyse and review information about the session by utilising self-reflection and feedback from participants and other staff involved in the session
- identify the effectiveness of the session in achieving its aims and goals
- review the key aspects of the session, eg the effectiveness of the activities and practices used
- identify their development needs and undertake further learning to address these.

Specifically, there are a number of things that a coach should consider when reviewing a coaching session. These include:

- **performance against pre-set goals** – coaches will have established a series of both short-term session goals and longer-term goals. An effective review of a coaching session will allow the coach to judge whether the short-term session goals were met and how far down the road towards the long-term goals the participants have progressed. Coaches should ask themselves whether the participants achieved the desired session goals and how any performance gains compare with the anticipated targets.

- **participants' progress** – review will help coaches to monitor their participants' progress and achievements over a period of time. An assessment of how well the participants are progressing will help inform the planning for future sessions. Coaches might ask themselves:
  - how well did the participants learn the techniques and skills introduced to them
  - what performance developments were evident for each participant
  - are the participants ready to progress within the next session?

chapter three

- **coaching ability** – review has a number of different dimensions to it and it is not just about reviewing how well the participants have done. There is also a need for a coach to review their own coaching ability and to reflect on the success, or not, of a coaching session in terms of their actions and behaviour. Coaches should consider:
  - what aspects of the session worked well
  - what aspects of the session worked less well
  - how the participants responded to the instructions given
  - whether the participants showed signs of boredom or restlessness
  - whether the coaching behaviour was appropriate.

- **future targets** – as previously suggested, reviewing is not just about looking back. It is also about forward planning and an effective review of a coaching session will help a coach set future goals and objectives based on the achievements and progress made by their participants.

Coaching is about working with people to try and help them improve. This principle should apply to coaches as well. Coaching practice will only develop if coaches themselves continuously strive to improve their own practice. This should be done through evaluating a coach's work in an objective way; treating failure and criticism as opportunities to improve.

The *UK Vision for Coaching* urges coaching as a profession to establish 'a culture and structure of innovation, constant renewal and continuous professional development' and it is the evaluation phase of the coaching process that can best stimulate this. Only through the self-identification of weaknesses can a coach begin to take responsibility for their own development and start the process of continuous professional development. Self-reflection can aid the identification of any gaps in skills and knowledge and lead to the quest to fill these gaps through taking part in coach education activities which aim to enhance coaching practice.

1 In pairs or a small group, discuss what a coach should consider when self-evaluating their coaching session.

2 List the people a coach should involve in the evaluation process.

chapter three

3.4 Long-term Planning

So far, much of what has been discussed with respect to the coaching process has focused on issues and actions associated with the delivery of a single coaching session. It is, however, unlikely that a single coaching session will have much of an impact on a participant's performance. Preferably, a participant will undertake a longer-term programme of development that is centred on achieving specific goals.

To achieve this, a coach should establish a long-term coaching plan that allows a participant to progress towards his goals in a stepwise manner. A good example of this would be the coach of an Olympic hopeful who may begin to develop a coaching and fitness programme for their participant one complete Olympic cycle (ie four years) in advance of the desired Olympic success. The coach will establish a four-year plan to prepare the participant for the next Olympics. Long-term planning does not always have to be for four years in advance. Most coaches who develop long-term plans will do so for a realistic period that is usually related to the season within their sport, or targeted towards some time-phased objective of their participants. Rugby coaches, for example, may plan the whole season's training programme from pre-season training in August through to the end of the season in May.

3.4.1 Periodisation

The concept of developing a long-term coaching programme that might take up to four years to complete may be daunting for some coaches. To make this a little easier to cope with, good long-term planners will adopt the principle of periodisation. Periodisation is about structuring a long-term coaching plan into smaller more manageable chunks of planned training. The aim of periodisation is therefore to divide the training period into smaller training cycles without losing sight of the ultimate training goals. Each smaller training cycle that is created should be progressive and should contain activities and training practices that build on the skills and fitness gained in previous cycles.

Figure 2 shows the typical structure applied to periodisation and highlights the different terms given to the smaller training cycles. The full training cycle is termed the **macrocycle** and is typically between one and four years in length. The macrocycle is split into smaller units, termed **mesocycles**. These will vary in length depending on the duration of the

chapter three

macrocycle. Typically, a one-year macrocycle is split into 12 month-long mesocycles. Within each mesocycle, there may be any number of smaller units – **microcycles** – which are typically one week in length. The microcycle is then made up of all of the individual coaching sessions that a coach plans.

chapter three

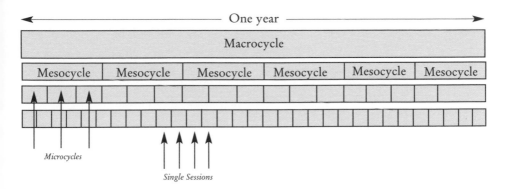

Microcycles

Single Sessions

Figure 2: Periodisation terminology and structure

The different training cycles identified within the macrocycle should be functional in that each should have a common theme. For example (Figure 3), if a cricket coach is planning a season based on the periodisation principle, they may identify that the single long-term planning unit – the macrocycle – will be 12 months in duration. This could be divided in to three mesocycles: *close season*, *pre-season* and *competitive season*. The focus of each mesocycle will be different and the aim of mesocycles is to distinguish the stage of training. The emphasis in the pre-season mesocycle will be on preparation and the development of appropriate fitness and skill levels for competition while naturally, the emphasis during the competitive mesocycle will be on playing and the refinement and maintenance of required skills and fitness levels.

If the coach identifies that the pre-season mesocycle (three-month duration) places an emphasis on the preparation and development of appropriate fitness and skill levels for competition, they may wish to sub-divide this mesocycle into more functional units: microcycles each of three weeks duration. Each microcycle may then place an emphasis on a particular element of pre-season work, eg development of underpinning aerobic fitness, development of sports-specific fitness, skill development and net/match practice.

chapter three

Each microcycle may then be further sub-divided into sessions. The coach will prepare a series of coaching sessions, each of which have specific sessional goals but also contribute to the goals for each microcycle, mesocycle and ultimately, the macrocycle.

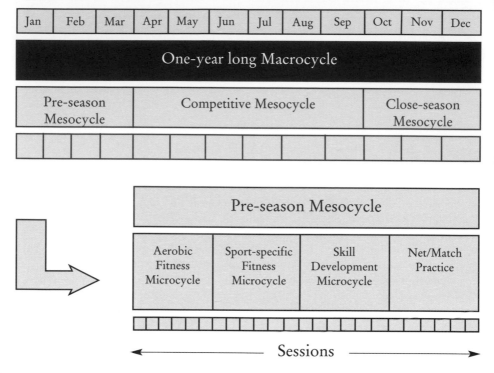

Figure 3: Example long-term plan for cricket

Long-term planning is therefore about structuring the training programme according to the identified long-term objectives, but with an emphasis on smaller units that allow more detailed planning to take place. A coach should aim to plan a coaching session so that it builds on the previous session and leads into the next while being part of the overall long-term plan.

chapter three

1 List and describe the different training cycles associated with a long-term coaching programme.

2 In pairs or a small group, discuss the benefits of periodisation within the long-term planning process.

chapter three

3.5 Summary

The coaching process is cyclical and requires the coach to undertake a number of actions in order to be effective. A coach must, with the aid of the participants, identify some measurable and achievable goals and identify a long-term strategy for achieving these goals. This long-term planning should identify all the key elements that need to be developed by assessing the participants' current standards of achievement and comparing them against the desired objectives. Having identified where each participant is heading on their coaching journey, the coach should set about planning how they are going to help the participant get there. This is achieved through identifying appropriate technical, tactical, physical and mental drills, practices and training methods to support the participants' development. The coach must then assimilate these activities into a plan, which should be structured according to appropriate timescales and broken down into small manageable cycles of training.

The ultimate unit of training will be a single coaching session and, while each of these will have session-specific objectives, a coach must also plan each session with the long-term objectives in mind. A coach should always view a single session as a part of the long-term development plan and never see a single session in isolation. Also, single coaching sessions should always be planned with the participants, the coaching environment and the available resources in mind. An effective coach will include activities appropriate to the needs and objectives of the session and be aware of the need to create a positive coaching environment.

A coach's plan should constantly evolve as each session is reviewed. It should be evaluated against the objectives of the session and both the short-term and long-term objectives of the participants. Any necessary changes for future sessions should then be incorporated and long-term plans adjusted accordingly.

chapter three

4.0 Where Next?

Sports coaching can be very rewarding and can help participants develop as individuals as well as sportspeople. For participants to benefit from the input of a coach the coach needs to adhere to some simple principles.

Coaching is about facilitating the development of others and coaches should develop their own style based on what and how they think coaching should be conducted. This should be built on solid foundations and reflect good practice by fulfilling the roles and responsibilities of coaching with integrity and respect. Coaches should always plan what they are going to do and base their actions on sound knowledge. Continual planning and reviewing of actions will allow for the successful implementation of the coaching process.

sports coach UK (scUK) offers a variety of workshops and resources related to the coaching process and the different coaching skills, styles and behaviours necessary for good coaching.

Resources

The following resources are available from **Coachwise 1st4sport** (tel 0113-201 5555 or visit www.1st4sport.com):

sports coach UK (2001) *Code of Conduct for Sports Coaches*. Leeds: Coachwise Solutions.

sports coach UK (2003) *How to Coach Children in Sport*. Leeds: Coachwise Solutions. ISBN: 1 902523 53 9.

sports coach UK (2003) *How to Coach Disabled People in Sport*. Leeds: Coachwise Solutions. ISBN: 1 902523 54 7.

sports coach UK (2003) *How to Coach Sports Effectively*. Leeds: Coachwise Solutions. ISBN: 1 902523 52 0.

sports coach UK (2003) *The Successful Coach*. Leeds: Coachwise Solutions. ISBN: 0 947850 16 3.

chapter four

sports coach UK (2003) *What is Sports Coaching?* Leeds: Coachwise Solutions. ISBN: 1 902523 51 2.

sports coach UK (2004) *How the Body Works in Sport*. Leeds: Coachwise Solutions. ISBN: 1 902523 55 5.

Stratton, G. (2004) *BASES Guidelines for Resistance Exercise*. Leeds: Coachwise Business Solutions.

Useful Contacts

sports coach UK

sports coach UK (scUK) works closely with national governing bodies to provide a comprehensive service for coaches throughout the UK. This includes an extensive programme of workshops, which have proved valuable to coaches from all types of sport and every level of experience. For more information about **scUK's** workshops and other services, contact:

> **sports coach UK**
> 114 Cardigan Road
> Headingley
> Leeds LS6 3BJ
> Tel: 0113-274 4802
> Fax: 0113-275 5019
> Email: coaching@sportscoachuk.org
> Website: www.sportscoachuk.org

chapter three

Child Protection in Sport Unit

Established in 2000 by Sport England in partnership with the NSPCC, the Child Protection in Sport Unit (CPSU) coordinates and oversees the development of child protection across sport.

> **Child Protection in Sport Unit**
> NSPCC National Training Centre
> 3 Gilmour Close
> Beaumont Leys
> Leicester LE4 1EZ
> Tel: 0116-234 7278/7280
> Fax: 0116-234 0464
> Email: cpsu@nspcc.org.uk
> Website: www.thecpsu.org.uk

National Governing Bodies

The national governing body for your sport or activity will give advice on coaching courses and other relevant information. National governing body contact details are available from:

> **Central Council of Physical Recreation (CCPR)**
> Francis House
> Francis Street
> London SW1P 1DE
> Tel: 020-7854 8500
> Fax: 020-7854 8501
> Email: info@ccpr.org.uk
> Website: www.ccpr.org.uk

chapter four